ISLAND OF THE DOLLS

Michael Dante was born in Wakefield in 1973. His poetry has appeared in many publications. His favourite subjects include human rights and mysticism. He has worked with some of Wales' most innovative writers and regularly performs his work with the Word Distillery Poets. He edited and contributed to the Word Distillery anthology, *Distillations*. His new book *Psychotropolis*, a powerful collection of poetry about human rights, will be published in 2017.

Praise for Michael Dante

Michael Dante has established himself as one of Britain's leading poets. He is a remarkable writer.

PIERRE SABAK, religious scholar and author of *The Murder of Reality* & *Holographic Culture*.

I have always admired his writing… he is an important British poet.

PROFESSOR DAVID PARRY, Fellow of the Royal Society of Arts, author of numerous books including, The Grammar of Witchcraft and Caliban's Redemption.

Michael Dante has a website: www.michaeldante.co.uk

ISLAND OF THE DOLLS

BY

MICHAEL DANTE

First published in 2017
by R. Haigh & Sons Publications

ISBN: 9780995682122

A CIP record for this book is available at the British Library

R HAIGH & SONS

FOR jeNNi HYAAT

A truly amazing poet and wonderful friend; over the years you've given me incredible support and encouragement. You've taught me so much and improved everything I've ever written. Thank you for your tireless proofreading. Every Tuesday in the 'Green Room' we miss your presence and our love goes out to you.

i take her hand wishing to reassure her. it removes itself from her body. i am talking to her. touching her wishing that she should answer me. but with each touch she is dismembered slowly. limb by limb. until headless... armless... legless...i carelessly lose my grip and she falls to the floor. there is a sharp noise – rather like broken glass. bending down i discover among the fragments a small doll... hairless... eyeless... and white from head to toe.

– peter carey, 'peeling'. collected stories –

die die die

TABLE OF SONNETS

CANTO 3:

SPIRIT OF THE ANACONDA

CANTO 1
MEXICO'S LAST SHAMAN

1.1. ON THE WATERWAYS

some of the fishermen and trappers think

that Don Julian Santana was mad.

They didn't know him like me. We'd drink

margarita or slam tequila in the sad

hours of the dawn. Looking back Don

Julian was a troubled man. He was a man

with many ghosts. Maybe he saw me as a son?

Anyway, I guess I had my own

reasons for being there. The last time

I had seen him; he had been weeping,

washing away his pain with Mexican wine.

He was upset about the girl and wept

    constantly about her. To console

    him I handed him a brand-new doll.

1.2. DON JULIAN

lifted his face from his palms and wiped

his nose across the soiled sleeve of his shirt.

He looked up from the dregs of his wine,

his smile the thinnest of cracks. Life had hurt

Don Julian, 'I don't know why she won't

leave me alone,' he whimpered. In the candle-

light he appeared almost as absent

as the statue on his altar. 'The Devil

has me,' he muttered to himself. I looked

around. There were maybe a hundred baby

dolls hung about his derelict

cabin – their skin freckled in mould. I could see

    around me a catacomb of dolls – most

      wore a rope collar or a wire noose.

1.3. SCARIEST

in his collection was the one he called
San Mónica – it was the damned strangest
thing I ever saw; it both appalled
and repulsed me. On the doll's twisted
lips was an ugly grin. This effigy wore
a black veil and a well-worn witches
cloak. She looked like a doll that years before
might have cost money. Dressed in the riches
of the rubbish tip, this small mannequin
bore a dozen or more rosaries around
her neck. Don Julian had given
her the title – '*Pequeño santo*.' On a brown
    candlelit altar it sat. He made her wear
    all kinds of crazy things; it looked vulgar.

1.4. A CLOWN

glared at me from above the altar Don
Julian had built from two upturned
orange boxes. To be honest, the clown
looked utterly wicked with its whitened
skull, half lost under a tumble
of matted dreadlocks, the circles
of its cheeks painted in a fickle
red. There was something menacing – cruel
about it…. At night, the island grew so dark
that it was easy to imagine some
terrible thing happening out in the thick,
tangled groves. As always, I'd come

> home an hour before nightfall as I know
> parts of this island are unsafe to go.

1.5. ÍSLA DE LA MU MUÑeCAS

was not exactly the 'floating garden,'

Don Julian had promised me. Rather,

I began to look at it as a prison.

Last April, one of his baby dolls fluttered

her plastic eyelids at me. I turned cold

and shuddered under the frozen sun.

I was sure she giggled. When I told

Santana, he nodded gravely. 'Listen

to me,' he said under his breath, 'that means

she's watching you. Be careful and stay away

from the canal.' The island was like a dream

from hell or a movie set, now decayed

    and lost to the ravages of time.

    And so Don Julian grew more solemn.

1.6. TeSHUiLO LAKe

was haunted, he was convinced of it.
'This place either accepts or rejects
you,' he once told me. To scare off spirits,
he put dolls everywhere. He had a complex
set of rituals to guard himself against
the *mal sucúbo*. Looking
back it was tragic. I guess I sensed
a change in his mood which began that spring –
a change that seemed one for the worse.
He became increasingly obsessed
with the dolls, and he felt that a curse
hung over the island. He seemed depressed,
    spending more time alone. 'You'll find,
    Amigo, this island plays tricks with your mind.'

1.7. SUPERSTITION

was Don Julian's best friend. He courted
her at every opportunity.
What played upon his mind and bothered
him most was the dead girl he
had found floating in the canal; he said
the dolls were really for her. He'd find them
on trash dumps. Often the things he said
never made much sense. The customs
he bastardised were a blend of Catholic
and Aztec rituals. 'You are Mexico's
last warrior-shaman,' I told him. 'Magic
Amigo,' he replied. His cigarette glowed
and a silver snake wriggled out of his mouth,
'*San Mónica* protects you – have faith.'

1.8.   FAITH

was something I lacked. I was a secret
born sceptic though I'd never have told
him that. Life by the water made him fret.
Sometimes I wondered about his old
stories, whether they were true? Perhaps he
was just lonely. I never asked him about
his life. I had heard once there had been
a woman, but that she had walked out
on him, and he hadn't been the same since.
There was a lot said about him which
wasn't true. Don Julian was convinced
that a number of spirits and angels watched
      him – that something evil lurked on that island:
      it dwelt by the water's edge near the woodland.

1.9. DeReLiCT

buildings and shabby outhouses were all
that remained of Don Julian's once thriving
business. The whole place had gone to hell.
Once he had made a successful living,
but since the girl had drowned, the tourists
had vacated the site. The old ferryman
eked out a life, doing a bit of this
and that, selling mainly medicines and
a little game to the fishermen.
The lakeside cabins were peeling,
and coloured flakes of lemon
paint had blistered away, revealing
    walls that had been stripped to the timbers
    by nature. The huts provided poor shelter.

1.10. THE ISLAND

looked like a sinister playground. Hundreds
of weathered dolls hung everywhere. Some
had been there for years. People said
Don Julian had picked up the first one
on the day he'd found the child
drowned. Her toy was floating in the water,
so he hung it in a bush. He'd compiled
a vast collection of dolls after
the girl's death. More and more, he assumed
a morbid countenance. The Island
terrified the locals. The old man exhumed
the dolls from dumpsites, trashcans, and land-

fill, he'd even fish them out of the canal
driven by his grief: his strange rationale.

1.11. OBSESSION

slowly poisoned his routines as Don

Julian became totally fixated

on the dolls. I could tell it got him down.

Dangling from the trees were decapitated

heads, severed limbs, lifeless staring eyes.

He told me one night that he could hear

voices from the water, he realized

from where the girl had drowned. They whispered

to him to come to the water's edge –

but he did not want to go. These voices

frightened him. When drunk, he made a pledge

to hunt down his nemesis –

    the *mal sucúbo.*   With one final attack

    into the heart of Hell, he'd send her back.

1.12. ANGeR

a latent rage and a sense of loss
seemed to drive Don Julian's increasingly
bizarre behaviour. Perhaps, it was because
he had a twisted past – a severely
wounded life which had left deep scars in his soul.
He tried to compensate for his pain
with a warped some might say,
perverted artistry. He spent more time on his own,
praying to St. Monica trying to rid
his conscience of some deeply ingrained hurt.
'You listen to those damned voices in your head,'
I told him, 'carrying all this pain and hate

    is bad. Why do you torture yourself?' I asked.

    His latest doll had a barbed wire mask.

1.13. THE DOLLS

were getting disfigured, he started to

crucify them to the trunks

of trees. He once told me that he had to

be strict with some of them. I think,

he was drunk that day; I could smell it

on him. I noticed some of the dolls

had scorch marks on their faces, and they emitted

the stench of burnt pulp. 'When the dolls

are sleeping, I finally get some peace,' he said.

I left him to himself; he was sulking,

punishing himself about the dead

child who'd drowned in the canal. 'That morning

    was twenty years ago,' I protested.

    But it was no good; he seemed agitated.

1.14. 'AT NIGHT

she comes alive,' said Don Julian,
his eyes sparkling with drink. 'I can't handle
it. She roams about the island. She's even
killed wild animals. Last night she strangled
a pelican. This jungle's full of spirits.'
He unscrewed the cap on his hipflask.
'Get off this island while you can, it's
no place for you Nicodemus.' Slowly, dusk
crept across the land, and it felt cold. The palms
were casting long shadows and a chill ran
deep in my bones. 'There's nothing in there to harm
us,' I said, pointing to the darkening ring
of palm trees. They stood like silent sentinels
guarding us – their fronds shadowed in purple.

CANTO 2
el MAL SUCUBO

2.1. SAN MONICA

fascinated Don Julian – she meant so much
to him. I could never work out why he
was so devoted to this Saint. He'd wash
her compulsively. Each morning, I'd see
him brush off army ants that crawled up
her face – her wig almost bald as he
combed the bugs from her scalp. With a cup
of rainwater, he would make himself busy
swabbing the Saint. He dressed her like the
Mother of God, transforming the doll
into a holy statue. On his knee,
the old shaman tenderly sat his idol.

Sometimes he'd veil her face with a net
praying to her as he smoked his cigarette.

2.2. A STRANGE SADNESS

had once more gripped Don Julian, it was
his constant companion. He was again
crying about the little girl; he was
always in tears. To me, he looked drained.
'Try to move on,' I said to him. 'There
is no point in blaming yourself.' He
took a gulp of wine and stared
into the hearth. 'This island killed her,' he
said, with a sour look on his face, 'here,
this holds a thousand prayers.' Don Julian
handed me a rosary. I saw the tears
well in his eyes. I noticed he'd given
    me the beads that usually
    St. Monica wore. 'It's your only

2.3. PROTECTION

from the *mal sucúbo.* She can't harm you
if you wear it.' He then took a silver
key out of his pocket and passed it to me. 'You
must hold onto this – this is the key to her lair,'
he whispered in a somewhat strange voice.
'She sleeps at the back of the boatshed; her hoard
is there. Trust in the power of God and rejoice
for *San Mónica* is on your side
Amigo.' Then from under his poncho
he pulled out a letter and handed it to me,
'only open it if the *mal sucúbo*
casts her black magic.' A drunken melancholy
    filled his voice, 'I need herbs this Easter to perform
    an exorcism to pacify her charm.

2.4. A CHiLDLeSS DeMON

haunts this old man.' He lowered his head,
his face now set deep in shadow.
'I am so sad *amigo*.' I nodded
in sympathy. Don Julian swigged a mouthful
of *Casa Madero*, 'the bastard
won't leave me alone...' I looked up
at the hundreds of mutilated
dolls and shivered. Many had been roped
up to a crossbeam that acted as a scaffold.
In the firelight their cracked faces melted
like molten wax. Don Julian rambled
on, his countenance now contorted:

    '*mal sucúbo* stole the life from this place.

    God I can still see her little face –

2.5. THe MURDeReD CHiLD

was strangled by her.' He spat into the fire –

the flames hissed and then a snarl

leapt across his lips, 'I'm going to make sure

I lift this serpent's curse. This quarrel

must be settled. If something bad happens,

promise me you'll leave?' I replied,

'it won't.' He leant over. 'Have we a bargain?'

he said seizing hold of my sleeve. I sighed.

'Nothing bad will happen....' 'I dreamed *Amigo*

I was like Jesus,' he said. 'I resurrected

from the dead and walked on water. Later, I will go

looking for her. I give you my sacred

    word – I will send the demon back

    and drive my tormentor into a dark

2.6. ReSTiNG PLAce...'

My head spun and I started to feel sick.
Don's Julian's bouts of drunkenness
and his increasingly erratic
behaviour concerned me – this odd axis
was in danger of unbalancing us both.
I was worried about my own slow slide
into alcoholism. In the undergrowth
of the decaying forest something had scared
Don Julian so much that it had
introverted his mind – turned him into
a recluse. Recently, I started
to wonder what could have happened to
    have made him like that. Also, I wondered
    to myself what the hell I was doing there.

2.7. THE SUCCUBUS

or *mal sucúbo* as he liked to call

it was a shapeshifting she-devil.

No one had seen it but him – she was small,

dark haired, and beautiful, with a strong will

and a quick mind. He knew she found men

attractive – but, she also had a liking

for the taste of human flesh. Once when

he had been young and fit, she had flung

herself into his arms. After seducing

him, she damned well nearly killed him. She'd

taunted him for years after. 'Once she chooses

her prey, she makes love to it and then she *feeds*.

    Her arms turn to green anacondas and coil

    around you – she has the heart of a gargoyle!'

2.8. A HUMAN SNAKE

was what he liked to call her, 'I stabbed her

Amigo, that's how I escaped,' he

said; 'sometimes she still whispers

she loves me, but I don't believe her,'

he then added, 'watch out, because

it only takes a kiss to steal your life-force,

just you remember *Amigo* – one kiss!'

The old man continued, 'I had intercourse

with her, and so I am damned, I tell you she

took half my soul.' He wiped his eyes, 'I fathered

her bastard, the *mal sucúbo* bewitched me.

In my youth, I was hypnotised by her

    beauty – for years I loved her. I was

    under her curse! Friday, I'll offer up some fishes,

2.9. SACRIFICE

a dove, maybe even a chicken. I fear

something untoward might happen:

I can sense that she is now near.'

He lowered his head, 'I'll do my bargain

in blood, cast the demon out tomorrow.'

I looked at St. Monica sitting upon

the upturned orange boxes. She seemed to glow

in the strange light fuming like a perverted nun.

Often I was sure that she watched

me through the tear in her veil. In

her long robes she looked more like a witch

than a saint. A demented jack-in-

    the-box seemed to be leaping out of her head:

    the clown hung from a nearby rope, green haired,

2.10. UGLY

and grinning, it added an eeriness
to the old man's creepy home.
I took a sip from my half-empty glass,
felt the warmth of the tequila worm
into my gut. Don Julian
looked up: 'she is the Patron Saint
of Disappointing Children.'
He focussed his eyes into a squint,
'I would have killed myself if it had not
been for her loving grace. May God bless
San Mónica, she saved my life.' I raised my shot
glass and said, 'I'll drink to that *Amigo*, God bless
the *"disappointing children"* of the world.'
'To *San Mónica Amigo*,' he echoed

CANTO 3
SPIRIT OF THE ANACONDA

3.1. LAST GOOD FRIDAY

I found the body of Don Julian

floating in the Xochimilico canal.

He was in the exact location –

the same channel where the little girl

had drowned twenty-two years earlier.

Next to his corpse floated a slaughtered

rooster. I fished out his bedraggled figure.

Don Julian looked slightly bewildered

as though he hadn't quite expected

death to strike him at that moment.

When I looked at the shaman, I shuddered.

I could tell his death had been recent –

 perhaps, in the last three hours, I saw

 rigor mortis creep into his eyelids and stiffening jaw.

3.2. IN THE WATER

I noticed the little doll I had given

him as a gift the night before – it floated

alongside the detritus. I reached in-

to the icy water, pulled out the doll and set

it onto the branches of a nearby

tree. My heart sank into the pit of my

belly, yet at least I knew inside

the old man was free. I prised

open his fingers, which were wrapped like

a boa constrictor around a small dead

dove, its wings crumpled. I noticed on its beak

a dribble of dark blood, which had

    embrowned its white bib. It took me a while

    to work out what had happened on this isle –

3.3. THE TRAGEDY

that had unfolded in Don Julian's life.

According to the letter he left for me,

the *sucúbo* and he were in love.

He said, he knew I would find it strange, he

told me: *love was a sacrifice*. He said,

she wanted *only* him and the girl. He had,

at first, attempted to use magic and tried

to drive her back into the water. He had

used the dolls to scare her off the island,

but no enchantment was as powerful

as a mother's bond. I was left stunned

by this new revelation. I couldn't construe

    the things he said, I started

      to fear he'd fallen under a wicked

3.4. CURSE

Anger is a poor mistress, he wrote, I
have lied to both you and to myself.
For years, I've tried to bury the truth. I
tell you *Amigo – we damn ourselves…*
Intern me at the back of the boatshed –
the spot where the grass grows yellow.
When I'm drunk ghosts fill my head,
I try to forget my past and fail to show
my true feelings. I haven't been sober
in such a long time – forgive me *Amigo* –
you have the key to the truth, it'll answer
everything, then it's time for you to go,
    your good friend Don Julian Santana…
    At the time, I had no idea

3.5. WHAT THE LETTER MEANT

I started to wonder whether I should
contact a priest or a medicine man
to finish Don Julian's botched
exorcism. I thought the old shaman's
soul had been stolen from him
by the *mal sucúbo* – I feared he
had succumbed to her vampirism.
Sometimes the truth can be hard to see –
living here makes one superstitious.
Indeed, I saw the *mal sucúbo*
with my own eyes. She had a lascivious
beauty. Don Julian was so
    right about her dark voluptuous locks,
    her full lips, her free and wanton looks.

3.6. I COULD SEE

why he loved her…. I shattered her skull
with my spade. I found the cash box at the
bottom of her grave. Inside the box – a bundle
of banknotes, some old photographs and the
truth behind Don Julian's doomed marriage.
What I saw horrified me – his suffering had
surpassed all comprehension or knowledge.
I discovered the grim and sad
truth when I dug Don Julian's grave.
Inside the cashbox were his diaries
and poetry. They explained his depraved
addiction: all he had suffered these
 lonely years, his manic-depressive swings –
 his self-hate and terrible yearnings.

3.7. THE DIARIES

were heartbreaking, I could scarcely read them

without welling up inside. Don Julian, once

was a happy man – yet through a gruesome

accident, his life unravelled. His conscience

gnawed at him like a wound that infected

his soul, which would not heal. His daughter

had drowned in the canal because of a stupid

mistake he and his wife had made. The danger

though obvious, had been unforeseen. On her

third birthday, Don Julian with his wife had

laid a picnic out for their daughter.

After too much wine, lemonade and cake they had

snuck away from the sleeping child and left her.

Don Julian swore that he could see her

3.8. FROM THE BUSHES

in harrowing detail, he described what

happened next. He remembered, his wife's body

slithering under his own as they made love. It

happened quickly. She writhed in ecstasy,

her hot breath on his cheek, her nails scratching

across his back and in his ears rang her

moans, her squeeze gently crushed him:

he felt the small death wash over him; then he heard

a terrible sound, his child screaming

for her papá. He ran to the edge of the canal,

half naked – his body gleamed

from the sparkle of lovemaking. Now the girl,

    was being rolled in the water by an anaconda:

    her limbs trapped in its coils. To add to the drama

3.9. HeR FATHeR

jumped into the canal armed with a knife;

meanwhile, the girl's bones broke apart

in their sockets and Don Julian's wife

screamed hysterically from the bank. His heart

smashed against his chest as he stabbed

the snake frenziedly. Suddenly,

the anaconda released its hold and

the girl's body floated free

from a froth of foam. From the shore her mother

sobbed and called out her child's name.

Don Julian dragged his lifeless daughter

back to the canal bank in a daze….

    He had recorded the event in his diary,

    The date read: Good Friday, 14th April 1911:

3.10. R.I.P.

As I read those old crumbling pages, I felt

his pain, his terrible loss. I sat

by the open grave to study his difficult

life, now told in the gruesome documents I sifted

through. Just as I thought it could not get worse,

I found out a number of things which disturbed

me and yet which also shed light on his curse.

Now I saw how events had merged

together in his brain. I traced his silent

obsession that had eaten into a lifetime

filled with pain. After a drunken argument

his distraught wife had drowned herself in the same

    spot of the canal as if to spite

    him. He wrote how betrayed and hurt he felt.

3.11. BY EASTER MONDAY

Don Julian's family was dead and he
was drunk. It wasn't long before he was
seen by the locals acting strangely
in the vicinity, fritting away his wages
and scaring off the tourists. His trade crashed.
From then on he wasted his life away – living
in a haunted funfair, floating on a trash
dump in the middle of Teshuilo Lake – ever in
a state of increasing squalor and rage…   I
read his strange story. Over the years the whiskey
turned sour. Growing ever bitter by
life's betrayal, he tried to bury his memory
    in a bottle, yet all the while his obsession
      kept him gripped in the thrall of addiction –

3.12. MORBIDITY

had dogged him from the day of his daughter's
death and the darkness of his loneliness
had seeped into his bloodstream – a mixer
that raced round his consciousness.
I saw how he had concocted the
story about the *mal sucúbo*. The dreams
which plagued his fitful sleep. Over time, love
turned to terror. He could not come to terms
with his wife's suicide – and yet,
he blamed her for the child's death:
so in his subconscious mind – when the night
crept softly, when the whiskey murmured and the breath
    of the jungle whispered in his soul – he
    would hear the light tread of his wife and see her

3.13. GHOSTLY

naked body and the timbers would creak
as she mounted his thighs – he'd lay there
petrified as she made love to him, wracked,
and mesmerised by fear, transfixed by her
stare: stiff as a corpse. There in the moonlight –
her arms writhing like green anacondas
and the night would swallow him like Fate ….
As I sat by his wife's grave, I read his diaries
and wondered what else I might find. Don
Julian was now rigid and his frozen lips
were cast into a downturned smile. The brown
earth-stained skeleton of his wife hid
    one more secret – through the green bars of her ribs
    lay a tiny skeleton curled up in a bony crib.

53

3.14. MARÍA-MAGDALENA

at the time of her death had been pregnant. I
looked through the photos of her sitting with
her young child, that's when I identified
the picnic hamper and saw his daughter's birth-
day cake. I inspected the picture of the child....
Way up high in the canopy a parrot screeched.
Above its perch, its plumage glittered like gold-
dust. I saw blood-red tips on its outstretched
tail feathers and the forest shivered as leaves
fluttered in the breeze and a large bird circled
like a rainbow-coloured angel over the grave.
When I realized what had happened on this secluded
   island a shudder ran down my spine
   for there, in *San Mónica's* shrine

3.15. MUMMiFieD

was a child! I recognized her from the
photograph taken on the day of her death.
I could not believe what I found at the
bottom of the cashbox – a rolled up Birth
Certificate, it read: *Monica Santana*,
14th April 1908. For all these years, Don
Julian had kept her in his cabin. His camera
caught her in life as form-
aldehyde had preserved her in death. Today
was her twenty-fifth birthday!
This new date had reopened another dark phase
in his mind, where cracks of sunlight were always
spoilt by rain, by the secret darkness
of his compulsions: his tormented conscience.

epilogue
behind the doll's mask

4.1. ✳

I placed Monica into her father's
arms and shovelled the dirt into my old
friend's face. The earth covered his daughter
and rustled like the mysterious folds
of a silk shroud, caressing her skin.
I buried Don Julian with two skeletons
and a virgin of sorrows. His only sin
had been that he had loved too much. On
the top of the grave, I placed the first
star-shaped flowers of spring – Mexican
orange blossom and the sweet scent burst
into the air like incense. Behind my back, broken
    dolls watched in the mangroves and from the red
    gum trees – haunted eyes bore down upon the dead.

4.2. I PRAYED OVER DON JULIAN

and the members of his family. I remembered
the strange custody battle he had
fought with his deceased spouse – how he hid
his embalmed daughter from the world; and his sad,
beautiful wife who had haunted him for twenty-two
years – stalking the island, searching only for her
daughter's mortal remains.... Such a worry
was bound to take a toll on him. I think he
thought, he could honestly nurse
his daughter back to life – maybe,
reclaim Monica from the curse
and release her from the *mal sucúbo*.

   I'm certain that was why he wired the jaws of the dead
   child shut – he was afraid of what she might have said!

4.3 IF ONLY THE DEAD COULD SPEAK!

Some believe Don Julian died of insanity,

they never knew him like I did, he

was a sweet and gentle man who struggled to free

himself from the bonds of his despair. He

tried to placate the spirit of his daughter with

more toys unable to let go of her corpse. Each

doll was a relic of his love. His last wish

was to be re-interred with his family.

'This place either accepts you or rejects

you Amigo,' he told me last spring.

After twenty years, this island finally accepted

him and his daughter, like his wife before him.

Last Good Friday, Don Julian was laid to rest.

He forgave his wife and broke the serpent's curse.

Nicodemus Sánchez, Easter Sunday,

Mexico City, 1934

DON JULIAN'S JOURNAL— 1911

LA MONECA

(QUEEN OF THE ISLAND OF DOLLS)

OUT ON THE WATERS OF XOCHIMILCO
WE LIVE ON A RAFT ON THE LAKE
A SMALL FLOATING GARDEN MADE YEARS AGO
BUT IT'S HOME TO THE FAMILY.

LEFT BY THEIR OWNERS — GATHERED BY ME
THEY ARE BROKEN. UNWANTED. UNLOVED.
I GIVE THEM ALL BEDS IN THE JUNIPER TREES
AND THEY WATCH FROM THE BRANCHES ABOVE.

LA MONECA. LA MONECA.
PORCELAIN — PERFECT AND SMALL.
LA MONECA. LA MONECA.
QUEEN OF THE ISLAND: THE ISLAND OF DOLLS.

Now i see her wherever i go
i visit the place i imagine she fell
and my dolls tell me things i can't know

La Moneca is queen of them all
and i keep her beside me all night
her body is blistered and peeling away
but she whispers to me that i'll be alright

if you should journey along this canal
and you hear a soft sound on the breeze
stay here and listen – you might hear a song
from my forgotten dolls in the trees.

KATHRYN ROBERTS & SEAN LAKEMAN'S ALBUM
'TOMMORROW WILL FOLLOW TODAY'

Die die die

Die die die

A SKETCH OF PAIN

DON julian SANTANA 1911

index

`Index of Titles and First Lines

some of the fishermen and trappers think   13

SPIRIT OF THE ANACONDA   39

that had unfolded in Don Julian's life.   43

was a child! I recognized her from the   55

was Don Julian's best friend. He courted   19

was haunted, he was convinced of it.   18

was not exactly the 'floating garden,'   17

was something I lacked. I was a secret   20

was strangled by her.' He spat into the fire -   33

was what he liked to call her, 'I stabbed her   36

were getting disfigured, he started to   25

were heartbreaking, I could scarcely read them   47

why he loved her.... I shattered her skull   46

74

BOOKS ALSO BY MICHAEL DANTE

Mirror of Enigmas: Reflections from the Xin Xin Ming

Mysterium

Psychotropolis

Orpheus: An Adaptation of Rilke

FORTHCOMING BOOKS BY R HAIGH & SONS BY THE SAME AUTHOR

Lao-Tzy's Tao Te Ching:
The path to Luminous Integrity

The Secret Code of the Tarot

The Green Man Alphabet

Oracle

A PROMISE TO OUR READER

R Haigh & Sons are a new and dynamic printing press. We aim to publish talented underground authors across the entire spectrum of poetry, philosophy and fiction. Our mission is to create quality books that will make a difference in people's lives. Above all, we value originality and craftsmanship.

Die die die

www.ingramcontent.com/pod-product-compliance
Lightning Source LLC
Chambersburg PA
CBHW071626040426
42452CB00009B/1514